MEMORIZE
· AND ·
MEDITATE

LAVONNE MASTERS

THOMAS NELSON PUBLISHERS
Nashville

Published in Nashville, Tennessee, by Thomas Nelson, Inc., and distributed in Canada by Lawson Falle, Ltd., Cambridge, Ontario.

Printed in the United States of America.

Scripture quotations are from the NEW KING JAMES VERSION of the Bible. Copyright © 1979, 1980, 1982, Thomas Nelson Publishers, Inc.

Library of Congress Cataloging-in-Publication Data

Masters, LaVonne.
    Memorize and meditate / LaVonne Masters.
      p. cm.
    Includes bibliographical references.
    ISBN 0-8407-3228-7
    1. Bible—Memorizing. 2. Meditation—Christianity. 3. Bible—
Devotional use. I. Title.
BS617.7.M373 1991
242—dc20   91-7605
                                                      CIP

In loving memory of my beloved parents
Alfred Benjamin Tosten, D.C.
and
Gertrude Merritt Tosten, D.C.
who taught me by example
to love the Scriptures.

ACKNOWLEDGMENTS

The Rev. Ron Masters, my husband, for his love and support.

Karen Westerfield and JoAnn Ellis, my daughters, for their prayers and reinforcement.

The Rev. Norman and Nathan Tosten, my brothers, for believing in me.

Jeanette Green, my sister, for simplifying the Memorize and Meditate concept.

Rev. Wayne and Carol Masters, my in-laws, for their prayers.

Lucy Corbin for taking time to critique this manuscript.

Evelyn Thorness for her special advice and for the quotes of her husband, the late Rev. Birger M. Thorness.

My friends for their prayers and encouragement.

Donna Woge for the idea of Memorize and Meditate for Kids.

Holly Burtt for her research and experience in child care.

The men and women who attended seminars and helped shape Memorize and Meditate.

Kin Millen for putting me in touch with the right people.

Carolyn Haynes for her insight and intuition.

The Rev. Carolyn Fritsch for her skill and sensitivity, which captured the essence of this manuscript.

Dr. Ronald Haynes, senior acquisitions editor at Thomas Nelson Publishers, for his hard work and creative approach, which breathed life into *Memorize and Meditate*.

Susan Salmon, editor at Thomas Nelson, for her expert finishing touches on this manuscript.

Thanks to you all.

CONTENTS

PART ONE: Memorize and Meditate   9

  1 Come Alive by the Word   11

PART TWO: The Five D's   21

  2 Step One: Decide the Method   23
  3 Step Two: Determine the Location   31
  4 Step Three: Discover the Content   37
  5 Step Four: Draw the Application   51
  6 Step Five: Do It   57

PART THREE: The Maintenance Plan   69

  7 Find a Partner   71
  8 Plan for Review   77
  9 Enjoy the Benefits   83

Appendix A   How to Teach Kids Memorize and
            Meditate   91

Appendix B   How to Start a Memorize and Meditate
            Club   103

Appendix C   Most Often Asked Questions   111

Notes   119

PART
ONE

MEMORIZE
AND
MEDITATE

CHAPTER 1

Come Alive
by the Word

You choose;
the Word empowers
your choice.

The flood surprised the residents of Rapid City, South Dakota. Twelve to fourteen inches of rain fell in less than three hours, causing the worst and most destructive flash flood in the history of that city. The force of those raging waters that night caused an estimated one hundred million dollars of damage. Two hundred thirty-eight people lost their lives—and among them were our three sons. As our family fled our home near the flooded creek, treacherous waters ensnared our vehicle. Hour after hour, we struggled against overpowering odds to hang onto life. My husband, Ronald, myself, and our two daughters, Karen and JoAnn, were miraculously spared.

But life stopped for us.

Our three sons—Stephen, twelve; Jonathan, eight; and Timothy, two-and-a-half—were gone. The pain was unbearable. We wondered if we would ever find our way out of this long dark tunnel.

In succeeding months, we learned to live one day at a time. Sometimes it was difficult to tell the days and the nights apart.

Two years passed. At first I tried adjusting to the imposed life change of loneliness without the boys by keeping busy with activities outside our home—Bible classes, shopping, eating out, anything to get away from home. When I wearied of this, I spent my energy working at home—baking, cleaning, reading, playing flute and piano. Eventually I drifted into watching endless game shows on TV. Then, one day I began to watch soap operas—with the sound turned down, you understand, so I could see how they decorated their homes, what clothes they wore, and how they styled their hair. The next day, I turned up the sound.

What was I doing? I asked myself. *Where was my life going?*

There had to be a change. I had experienced the pain of sorrow long enough, and I knew I could not exist like this forever. Inside I felt as though part of me had died. My mind seemed dead. I had stopped trying. I had lost hope. I knew better than this.

In the next few months, I grappled for a solution. I had to make some positive choices. First, I decided to take responsibility for the quality of the rest of my life. It began to dawn on me that God could not do that for me.

Second, I chose to reprogram my thoughts. My negative thoughts, depression, and aimlessness controlled my life and resulted in dysfunctional behavior of many wasted hours in front of the TV. I was raised in a Christian home by parents who studied and lived by the Scriptures. So, technically, I realized that the Bible had the answer for my life. But I had to put this knowledge into action. So I began to fill my mind with the Word by memorizing and meditating.

The result? My life changed. The transformation soon became obvious to those around me: Instead of sorrow, depression, emptiness, and purposelessness, my life was marked by healing, peace, creativity, and purpose. Memorizing and meditating revolutionized my world so that I was able to gain perspective on all that had happened in the previous months. I came out of my pit and felt and looked alive again.

I have continued to use Memorize and Meditate for the more than fifteen years since I lost my three sons. I have refined the program since then and have taught it to various groups. Not every event of my life has been perfect since I have begun to use the program; however, I can tell a difference in my response to daily pressures and frustrations when I am consistently using the program, and even in times when I have temporarily put the program on hold.

I am often reminded of the frantic pace of life we all lead when I watch the seagulls down on the waterfront in Seattle. Our family's favorite restaurant is a fish bar, where we buy fish and chips and sit outside on the pier to eat. We always share our lunch with the seagulls that float and swoop nearby.

The last time we were there, I noticed some interesting things about the gulls. The seagulls that made the most noise with their constant squawking never seemed to get much food. But the ones that were quiet and determined and glided above the others had the greatest opportunities to feed.

So it is with us when we memorize and meditate on God's Word. We become quiet and peaceful in our spirits and gain God's perspective on our circumstances so we can rise above the tensions of family demands, career pressures, and juggling priorities. The effects of Memorize and Meditate create a cycle: When we become quiet and peaceful in our spirits, we find time for the food of the Word of God. And when we find time for the food of the Word of God, we become quiet and peaceful in our spirits. Through memorization, we retain God's Word, and through meditation, we grasp God's Word so we can grow and mature.

WHAT IS MEMORIZATION?

Memorization is the first step in your pilgrimage into God's Word. Often people say to me, "I can't memorize anything." The fact is, however, that consciousness without memory is insanity. Thus, as sane beings, we memorize what we want to, and we remember it. You may not like the idea of memorization, but don't be afraid of the word *memorize*. I'm not fond of it, but I use memorization as a means to an end. You can effectively meditate only when you've memorized.

Two excellent Scripture verses pertaining to memorization are:

Your word I have hidden in my heart,
That I might not sin against You. (Ps. 119:11)

Let not mercy and truth forsake you;
Bind them around your neck,
Write them on the tablet of your
  heart. (Prov. 3:3)

WHAT IS MEDITATION?

Meditation is getting to know God better, spending time with him. If you love someone, you want to be alone with that person. If you love the Lord, you want to spend time alone with him.

When we meditate on Scripture, we fill our minds with God's Word and let the truth sink into our hearts. We allow our Father to speak to us in the depths of our souls. We commune with him, and then act upon the instruction of his Word.

Some people, however, are skeptical of meditation. So let's look at the two Hebrew words used in the Old Testament for *meditate* and their meanings.

The first Hebrew word for *meditate, hâgâh,* appears in Joshua 1:8: "This Book of the Law shall not depart from your mouth, but you shall meditate [*hâgâh*] in it day and night, that you may observe to do according to all that is written in it. For then you will make your way prosperous, and then you will have good success." *Hâgâh,* (pronounced haw-gaw′), means to mutter and murmur, to speak in a low inaudible voice with oneself.[1]

The second Hebrew word for *meditate, sîyach,* is in Psalm 119:15: "I will meditate [*sîyach*] on Your precepts, / And contemplate Your ways." *Sîyach* (pronounced see′-akh), means to ponder or muse and pray. Someone said it can be likened to a pilgrimage into God's Word.

The *Random House College Dictionary* defines *meditate* as "to reflect, contemplate, a thinking over." When we look up the word *contemplate,* we find that it means to consider thoroughly, to think fully or deeply about.

The Scripture verses below illustrate the positive results of meditation. Words and thoughts become acceptable to the Lord, there is joy in the Lord, and finally, there is transformation by the renewing of the mind.

> *Let the words of my mouth and the*
> *   meditation of my heart*
> *Be acceptable in Your sight,*
> *O Lord, my strength and my*
> *   redeemer.* (Ps. 19:14)
>
> *May my meditation be sweet to Him;*
> *I will be glad in the Lord.*
> *   (Ps. 104:34)*

COME ALIVE BY THE WORD

*Be transformed by the renewing of your mind,
that you may prove what is that good and
acceptable and perfect will of God.*
(Rom. 12:2)

Jesus said, "When you pray, go into your room, and when you have shut your door, pray to your Father who is in the secret place; and your Father who sees in secret will reward you openly" (Matt. 6:6). You will most often meditate in private, but the Lord will reward you openly. Out of emptiness, loneliness, and restlessness you will enter into richness, creativity, and new potential. In fact, you will have the most productive creative thoughts when you are in a quiet place lying down, completely relaxed. Start by breathing deeply. Slowly will your whole body to unwind. Then begin to think about the verses you are currently memorizing.

I vividly remember enjoying eating black walnut cake with my family when I was growing up in Iowa. But we had to go through a process to enjoy that cake. First, we would go into the country and pick walnuts from the ground under those huge trees. Then when we arrived home, my sister, Jeanette, and I would sit out in the backyard and take the hulls off the nuts. Next, we would bring the nuts into the house to crack the shells. The best part of the process was picking the meat out of the shell. It was difficult for us to leave enough for the cake. But later, when the aroma of that luscious dessert permeated the kitchen and we tasted the masterpiece, we agreed it was worth all the effort.

One of our greatest joys as believers comes when we can share together the positive results of practicing Scriptures in our lives. However, without the efforts of memorization and meditation, this joy is unattainable. First, we must commit to choosing the verses and creating a schedule. Like picking and hulling nuts, this is not always pleasant. Second, we must memorize—crack the shell of the verse. This is the first necessary energy for going below surface-meaning to reach depth-meaning. Third, we pick the meat out of the verse and eat it—that is, we meditate on the verse, wherein we taste the deep truths of Scripture and savor them one at a time. And finally, we are able to practice the Scriptures and enjoy the results; we are able to make the cake and eat it, too.

We may religiously take our Bible to church every Sunday, but not until we read it, study it, and devour it does it become a part of us. Then we can think about those words at any time. We can live in the atmosphere of that Book anywhere. If our Bible remains unused, it is not ours. When we take the contents within, it becomes ours.

My prayer is that you will realize new growth and the transformation of your world as you begin to memorize and meditate on God's Word.

In part two, I will present the five D's of Memorize and Meditate:

- **Decide the method**
- **Determine the location**
- **Discover the content**
- **Draw the application**
- **Do it**

Then, in part three, we will discuss ways I've found helpful for you to remain consistent in the program for the rest of your life.

PART TWO

THE FIVE D'S

✦ CHAPTER 2 ✦

Step One:
Decide
the Method

Faith

comes by

the Word.

In my fifteen years of using, then teaching, the Memorize and Meditate program, I have discovered five tried and proven methods of memorization. It may be possible that you will be able to use all of the methods at one time or another in your memorizing. Choose the method or methods you feel most comfortable with, the ones that work best for you. And in all of your memorization, remember these two key principles: (1) learn every word and (2) finish memorizing the portions you have started to memorize.

You haven't learned a verse if you haven't learned it perfectly. Learn all the words. Check yourself for errors by placing a card over the verse and moving the card down one line at a time as you say the verse, covering what you're saying and uncovering it to check.

Also, finish what you start. This is important to your feeling of self-worth and a sense of accomplishment, and it can help you to develop more discipline. Do not jump around from chapter to chapter or book to book. Instead, if you start to memorize fifteen verses or a chapter or a book, stay with that section until you've memorized it.

METHOD #1: REPEAT THE VERSE

Devising elaborate schemes to help you memorize occasionally backfires. Repetition is the most common, most reliable memorization technique, with no tricks to learn. There are several important steps to help you with this approach.

1. *Read* the verse at least three times to imprint it in your mind. Block out everything else—turn off the

radio or TV, lock the door, turn on the answering machine—and concentrate on what you're reading.

Benefit also from "Space Learning" which is simply learning a little now and a little throughout the day. It is another means of repetition. Every time you say a verse, repeat it three times, wait a space of time, then repeat the verse three times again. The system works like this: verse three times—space—verse three times—space—verse three times—space—until you feel you have learned it. The spaces can be for any length of time, from one minute to several hours. Each time you say your verse after the space of time, a new imprint is made on your brain. You can say the verse three or thirty times without a break, and it will make only one impression in your mind. What makes this system effective is the fact that you must come back to the verses after each space of time.

2. *Visualize* the verse. Look closely at the verse on the page of your Bible. Notice the line breaks, the hyphenated words, and the large words. Then close your eyes and try to *see* the verse in your mind's eye. Be sure to use *one* Bible for your memorization and meditation so you will be able to envision the location of all the verses on the pages of your Bible: how far down on the page the chapter starts, approximately where each verse is located—whether it is at the top of the page, in the left-hand column, or half-way down the page in the right-hand column. When I started with Memorize and Meditate I used one Bible when I was at home and a different Bible when I was away from home. As a result, the pictures of the verses became confused in my mind's eye, and it was difficult for me to retain what I had memorized. I depended on the mental image of the verses for recall.

Using two Bibles, I found I had double vision of every verse in my mind. So stay with one Bible.

3. *Vocalize* the verse. Saying and hearing the verse said out loud makes a double impression on the mind. Always make use of this procedure.

4. *Write* the verse three times. It is not necessary to write out every verse you memorize (though there are those who do), but when you can't seem to memorize a verse, this gives you a breakthrough. Any activity that brings more of your whole person into the learning process will help you to learn more quickly and retain information longer. Thus using the muscles in your arm and hand to write is one more aid for committing verses to memory.

5. *Stretch* your mind. As you repeat a verse during the day, make yourself recall as much as possible of the verse before you check yourself in your Bible. Try first to visualize the big words of the verse in your mind, and then do the same with the small words. This may be an unpleasant strain at first, but it is necessary for the development of the memory section of your brain, which possibly hasn't had much of a workout. Don't worry or get uptight. If you relax, the words will come to you.

METHOD #2: FORM ACRONYMS

Use the initial letters of major words to form a word or an acrostic. When I was memorizing Ephesians 4:31 ("Let all bitterness, wrath, anger, clamor, and evil speaking be put away from you, with all malice"), using this method helped me to learn it with little difficulty. The key words of the verse are *bitterness, wrath, anger, clamor, evil,* and *malice.* The first letter of each word put together forms *BWACEM*. Because the acronym is so odd sounding, I probably will never forget the verse. You also can create a sentence with those same letters: By Watching After Children Enjoy Mania. I won't vouch for the sentence structure; you are limited with the letters. But the zanier the sentence, the longer you'll be able to remember it.

METHOD #3: ASSOCIATE

Another way to memorize is by association. You can use either mental pictures or categories to help you with this method. When you link ridiculous mental pictures with each verse, your memory of the verse will be more permanent. Jerry Lucas, co-author of *The Memory Book,* says, "You can remember any new piece of information if you associate it with something you already know or remember."[1] This is very successful for many people, and it is a procedure that may aid you. If you find that you're spending more time trying to dream up the mental pictures than you are memorizing the verse, this method is probably not for you.

Another way to associate is to categorize. If someone asks you to buy a list of items at the store, you can group them according to where you'll find them in the store so you can remember them more easily. For example, you may group the items according to milk products, frozen foods, or salad ingredients.

You can apply this memory technique when you're memorizing a chapter of Scripture as well. If you were to memorize Philippians 1, you would note how many verses were included in the salutation. Then, you would examine the prayer following the salutation and ask yourself the main points of the prayer. As you write these down, you might group them as follows: praise, character development, spiritual development. Choose categories you think describe the verses. These are points and phrases to help you memorize. You don't need to consult a commentary to help you categorize.

METHOD #4: RECORD ON CASSETTE

Many people today enjoy using a tape recorder to assist in memory work. Record the portion of Scripture you are memorizing and listen to it several times. (You may want to use some means of repetition, such as those described under Method #1, to help you.) Then, as you begin to say the verse, play back the recording to check yourself. You may choose to record one verse several times, or you may want to record a whole chapter. It will possibly be more pleasant for you to have a member of your family or a friend record the verses for you, so you can listen to someone else's voice instead of your own. An excellent time to play recordings is just before you go to sleep at night. This fills your subconscious mind with the Word.

METHOD #5: SING SCRIPTURE

As a young girl at home, one of my tasks was to wash or dry the dishes with my sister. To make the work seem lighter, we made up opera-style melodies to communicate everything we wanted to say to each other.

STEP ONE: DECIDE THE METHOD

"Jeanette, will you wash off the table?"

"Not now, I'm scrubbing this pan."

I'm sure we made a fantastic amount of noise. I don't know how the rest of the household could stand it. But it was pleasant for us, and in no time we were through with the dishes.

When you adapt your verses to familiar melodies, or to melodies you create, the verses form a permanent impression in your mind. Just as learning the ABC's to a tune inspired quicker learning when you were a child, so also you'll notice that learning your verses to a tune will be quicker. You'll find the experience of singing your verses especially uplifting when your spirits are down. The tunes need not be works of art, and you need not be an excellent singer. This is a great way to enjoy yourself and learn at the same time.

CHAPTER 3

Step Two:
Determine
the Location

You are
---
renewed
---
by the Word.

God gave each of us a marvelous computer for storing information: the brain. The brain contains enough potential connections to receive *ten new items* of information per second. Everything we do every moment of our lives is controlled by its billions of components.[1]

With this wonderful technology at our disposal, filling our minds with large portions of the Word—God's thoughts—will enable us to use these stored thoughts for our benefit, in the good times and in the hard times.

MEMORIZE LARGE SECTIONS

The first step in determining the location of passages is to consider memorizing large sections of Scripture. From experience, I recommend that you learn no less than fifteen verses of a chapter or learn complete chapters or books rather than random verses. Most of us will admit that it is more difficult to remember verses and their location if they have been selected at random. I remember being handed two pages of verses to learn in a Sunday school class as a teenager. I memorized all the verses, but I had trouble recalling where each verse was found. To this day, I can't match some of those verses with the right book or chapter.

When you memorize a large segment of a chapter or a book, you will be able to see in your mind's eye the location of every verse and every chapter because of the amount of time you have spent there. I suggest that you start with a half chapter, a small chapter, or a small book. When you finish memorizing the smaller portion, you will have confidence to tackle the larger portions.

STEP TWO: DETERMINE THE LOCATION

Don't let the large sections of Scripture scare you. Memorize each chapter, one verse at a time. Learn verse one; then verses one and two; then one, two, and three. Always strive to quote the text you've learned along with each new verse you memorize.

PRAY FOR DIRECTION

The second step is to pray for direction to the section most beneficial for you. Simply ask God to guide you to the chapter or book you are to meditate upon. Most people, after praying about it, do feel inclined or impressed upon to turn to a specific chapter or book God knows they are going to need in their lives. I started with Philippians, then went on to Ephesians. Both books were exactly what I needed for that time in my life. Margaret began memorizing and meditating on Psalm 91 as God directed her. Of course, she did not know what life held for her. Three weeks later her husband died suddenly in the night from an aneurysm. She found him gasping in a chair and tried to revive him. But her efforts failed. She called her daughter for help, then the ambulance, but he was already gone. There was nothing she could have done.

The night of the funeral there was a terrible wind and rain storm. The enfolding words of Psalm 91 took away all fear. Before she started memorizing this psalm, she was extremely fearful. She even checked under beds to make sure no one was there. For several months she continued quoting the words of the psalm before going to sleep at night and when she awakened in the night. Now she knew that God was going to take care of her. The comfort and healing she derived from the Scriptures could not have been obtained from any other source.

After praying about what to memorize, if you are still not certain where to begin, start memorizing a chapter that has always been your favorite or select a chapter in the area of your need. Or use the list of chapters and books below to give you some ideas. There are so many excellent Scriptures to memorize and meditate on. But keep in mind that you want to meditate on the Word that will relate to your life now and in the months to come for maximum effect.

HALF CHAPTERS

Proverbs 31:10–31; Matthew 5:1–26; Matthew 6:1–18; John 3:1–21; Romans 8:26–39; Ephesians 5:17–33.

SMALL CHAPTERS

Psalm 1, Psalm 2, Psalm 23, Psalm 100, Psalm 121, Isaiah 55.

SMALL BOOKS

Philippians, Colossians, 2 Thessalonians, 2 Timothy, Titus, Philemon, 2 Peter, 2 or 3 John, Jude. Each of these books has no more than four chapters. You will be able to learn them in a year or less.

CHAPTERS

Psalms 1, 23, 25, 37, 91, 143—God's care
Psalm 119—Love of the Word
Psalms 24, 33, 34, 126, 138, 150—Praise and encouragement

STEP TWO: DETERMINE THE LOCATION

Proverbs 2—Wisdom
Proverbs 31—A virtuous wife
Isaiah 40—Comfort
Isaiah 53—Redemption
Jeremiah 1—God's call
Matthew 5, 6, 7—Practical Christian living
Matthew 13—Seven parables of Christ
John 3—Born of the Spirit
John 14—Peace
John 17—Christ prays for us
Romans 4—Faith
Romans 8—Victorious living
Romans 12—Know yourself
1 Corinthians 13—Love
1 Corinthians 15—The Resurrection
Ephesians 5—Walk in love
Ephesians 6—The armor of God
Philippians 4—Positive thinking
Hebrews 11—Faith
1 John 3—Love

BOOKS

Proverbs—Wisdom
John—The power of the Son of God
Romans—Doctrine and Christian duties
Ephesians—Unity of believers
Philippians—Positive thinking
1 Timothy—Counsel to a young pastor
James—Good works
1 Peter—Victory over suffering
1 John—Fellowship and love

THE FIVE D'O

CHAPTER 4

Step Three: Discover the Content

The Word

is your contact

with God.

We are so familiar with feeding on someone else's gleanings that many people are under the impression that only ministers and Bible teachers are qualified to discover deep truths from the Word. Actually, anyone who desires to may do so. When you start feeding yourself, you'll never be completely satisfied with anything else. Nothing equals a fresh thought from God for you alone. The first time I uncovered a truth for myself, I felt a sunburst over my spirit. Psalm 46:10a says, "Be still, and know that I am God." God wants us to slacken our pace and know—care, acquaint, recognize—him. God yearns for an intimate relationship with each one of us. In the rest of this chapter, we'll walk through the basic steps of meditation together as we meditate on Romans 12:2. It takes a few years to develop the art of meditation. But in time, you'll acquire a few of your own unique methods, which you'll use as well as the ones included here.

GATHER RESOURCES

Before I give you the skills for meditation, you will need to gather some materials for assistance:

1. Bible
2. concordance
3. dictionary
4. index cards
5. card file box
6. guide cards

Resource Books. The first book needed is a Bible.

STEP THREE: DISCOVER THE CONTENT

Now is the time to purchase a new Bible, if you have been considering it. Remember, start this program with one Bible so you will remember the location of all the verses and chapters you will learn.

I have found the King James Version easier to remember than other translations, because the more formal English sticks in my mind longer than the modern English translations. If you can't memorize the King James, try the New King James Version.

The second important book you will need is a *Strong's Exhaustive Concordance* containing glossaries of the Hebrew and Greek words used in the Bible. This will be used in researching words from Scripture.

The third necessary book is a dictionary for researching words in the definitions of the Hebrew and Greek glossaries.

If you desire more resource material, you can use several different Bible translations, word meaning books, and commentaries.

All of these resources should be available at your local Christian bookstore. The books you use are a matter of personal preference. But the three basic books for meditation are a Bible, a concordance, and a dictionary.

RECORD YOUR THOUGHTS

As you discover the content of the verses you are memorizing, you will want to record the definitions of the words and any thoughts or applications the verses may have for your life. You can easily use a journal for this, but I suggest that you use index cards. They are easy to organize, and you can carry them with you in a briefcase, handbag, suitcase, or backpack. (When you carry cards with you, you can write down meditative thoughts whenever they come. A good thought's arrival cannot be predicted, but if you have cards with you, it won't be lost.)

You can purchase 3" x 5" index cards in a variety of colors. You can use a different color for each chapter or for each book, or, if you're a purist, you may prefer white. (White cards are also cheaper.)

Keep all your cards together in a card file box. Approximately four hundred cards fit into one metal box. Label the outside of the box and store it on a bookshelf.

Use guide cards marked with chapters to separate your chapters and books within your card file boxes for convenience when you need to find a card.

You can also buy a card holder for carrying your cards with you, or you may use a billfold, a checkbook, a date book, or anything else you have. I carry up to forty cards of the current chapter I'm working on in my date book. When I am finished with that chapter, I take the cards out and store them in my card file box.

When you carry your cards with you, you can read them anytime you're down or need encouragement. If someone asks you about your cards, it will give you an opportunity to tell that person what you are doing and what it has done for you.

UNDERSTAND THE MEANING

The first step to discovering the content of a verse is to understand the meaning of the words and the verses. You will not want to research every word, only the ones you are curious about. Some verses will have no words to examine; others will have many words to examine in depth. But be aware that some of the verses you think have little to uncover may be rich in content. You may even discover deep truths in salutations.

In the New King James Version of the Bible, Romans 12:2 says, "And do not be conformed to this world, but be transformed by the renewing of your mind, that you may prove what is that good and acceptable and perfect will of God." Before you begin to research the important words in this verse, on one of your index cards write the number of the verse at the top left-hand corner. (See the sample card on page 49.) It is not necessary to memorize the number of each verse unless you desire to do so, but writing the number helps you to organize the cards in your file box.

Then, write the verse, in this case Romans 12:2, at the top of the card. Write only one verse per card, and write the verse exactly as it appears in your Bible, including the same word and sentence breaks. To see the verse on your card exactly as you see it in your Bible will help you to recall the verse better.

Be sure that you have the correct meaning of verses, taking careful note of all words and punctuation. For instance, from the Bible we read in Ephesians 4:28a, "Let him who stole steal no longer, but rather let him labor, working with his hands." This could be misquoted as, "Let him who stole steal; no longer let him labor with his hands." Notice that some of the words have been left out and the punctuation has been changed. Thus knowing every word and every verse in every chapter is imperative to correct meditation. Be careful of yielding to the temptation of leaving out verses because they aren't particularly interesting.

For word research, use the concordance first, then the dictionary. *Strong's Concordance* is relatively easy to handle with only three essential parts: the main concordance, a Hebrew dictionary, and a Greek dictionary. The main concordance contains all the key words of the Bible in their context. The Hebrew dictionary includes definitions for Old Testament words because it was originally written in Hebrew. The Greek dictionary includes the definitions for New Testament words because it was originally written in Greek. (Although *Strong's Concordance* is keyed to the King James Version, you can use it with the New King James Version, and you can use the Greek and Hebrew dictionaries with any translation.)

In order to research a word with the *Strong's*, find the *exact* word in the main concordance as it appears in the text of the translation you are using. For instance, in looking up the word *conformed* (not *conform* or *conforming*, but *conformed*), you will notice a number by the reference, number 4964. (If there is no number by the reference, there is no Hebrew or Greek word for it.) Then find number 4964 in the Greek dictionary (this is a New Testament word) to discover the original definition of the word *conformed*. You will find the Greek word suschēmatizō, which means "to fashion alike."

You also can use other Hebrew and Greek dictionaries available, such as *Vine's Expository Dictionary of Old and New Testament Words, A Reader's*

Hebrew-English Lexicon of the Old Testament, and
A Reader's Greek-English Lexicon of the New Testament.

On your index card, under Romans 12:2, record the Greek meaning for the word *conformed.* If you are a Hebrew or Greek scholar, you may want to include the Hebrew or Greek word on the card as well as the meaning.

When you find words in the Hebrew or Greek definitions you'd like to examine further, you can turn to your dictionary. If you look in the dictionary to learn the meaning of the word *alike,* found in the Greek definition of *conformed,* you might find:

> **a·lik'e** *(a·līk') showing no marked or
> important difference.*[1]

(You could also look up the word *fashion,* if you desired to think more about this verse.) Jot down on your index card the definitions of the words you look up in your dictionary.

From the definitions in the concordance and the dictionary, we begin to understand that, in the first part of this verse, Paul is warning us against having no marked or important difference from the world. You can see how using the concordance along with the dictionary opens up new avenues of thought. The dictionary is indispensable in the meditation process.

If you want to study words in more depth, you can use various Bible translations, word meaning books, and commentaries. You may want to transcribe quotations from these other sources onto your index cards. This is an optional step, but other references

---

often shed light on the verses you're meditating on. If you are stumped by a verse, consciously gather all known data through the analytical processes available in these books, and let your subconscious transform the information into useful applications. Take advantage of the hours of research done by other authors.

In copying quotations, use abbreviations for the sources of information on your cards. For instance:

> **SC**—*Strong's Concordance*
> **WD**—*Webster's Dictionary*
> **NRSV**—*New Revised Standard Version*
> **WM**—*Word Meanings in the New Testament*
> **MHC**—*Matthew Henry's Commentary*

Later, as you review memory verses, you may want to return to the references you used to answer new questions you may have.

ASK GOD FOR ENLIGHTENMENT

The second step in meditation is to ask God for enlightenment. Dare to ask God for practical truths to be used in your life, your business, and your relationships.

In Numbers 12:8 we read of the Lord speaking openly with Moses because Moses was at home with him. When meditating, feel free to ask questions openly. God does not mind. That's how we learn. As you meditate on Romans 12:2, you may want to ask

God to help you see how you are *alike* the world and how you are different. You may ask him to help you understand what it would mean for you to be "transformed by the renewing of your mind."

Below the definitions you've written on your index card (or on the back of the card, if necessary), try to write down the thoughts you have about each verse. Often, great thoughts are born out of seemingly insignificant thoughts, so write down everything. Then state how you can apply this verse to your life. Once you write your thoughts and applications, you will not easily forget them, and you can refer to your card whenever you wish to refresh your memory.

You will not write word definitions for every verse because some verses will not have any words that need to be researched. But you should always record your meditations and applications for every verse. If you see that you haven't written anything on one or more of the cards, reread the verses and try to think of something to write about. Recording your thoughts on each card helps to slow you down so you can meditate on every verse. Some verses may need more than one card to contain all the research and meditations.

Remember, the word *meditate* means to mutter and murmur. So for further enlightenment, try self-verbalization. Pretend you're explaining your Scriptures to someone. Say them out loud. Talk to yourself. If you'd feel more comfortable with an audience, your cat or dog can be very loyal and attentive. Children under five years old use self-verbalization to help reinforce thoughts they have that aren't fully formed. When they become older they quit because of peer pressure. We adults, however, can benefit in our meditation by reviving the technique of self-verbalization.

PARAPHRASE

The third step of meditation is paraphrasing. Simply restate the verse, substituting personal pronouns, your name, and word meanings you discovered when you looked up the Hebrew, Greek, and dictionary definitions.

For example, the paraphrase of Romans 12:2 might read: "And, (your name), don't allow yourself to be made to be like this world, having no marked difference, but be changed by having your mind made new, by beginning to think differently so that you may prove (be an example of) what is the good, acceptable, perfect will of God."

You will notice that I didn't research all the words, but only the ones that were important to me; I made substitutions. Some individuals like to paraphrase every verse, because it helps them to clarify and personalize the verse, and it helps to practice the Scripture.

REMEMBERING THE DETAILS

As you've gone through the basic steps of meditation, you've been using your index cards to record the verse and your thoughts and the applications you've made. The illustration of a meditation card on page 49 will give you another idea of what your cards will look like. Remember, your cards will include six basic elements:

1. The number of the verse.
2. The verse exactly as it appears in your Bible.
3. The Hebrew or Greek definitions of the significant words in the verse, the words you've researched.
4. The dictionary definition of the words from the concordance.
5. Your thoughts about the verse and applications of the verse to your life.
6. Quotations from other sources—other translations, word-meaning books, commentaries.

SAMPLE CARD—FRONT AND BACK

2. And do not be conformed to this world,
but be transformed by the renewing of
your mind, that you may prove what is
that good and acceptable and perfect
will of God.

SC conformed - suschēmatizō "to fashion alike"
WD alike - "showing no important difference"
SC transformed - mĕtamŏrphŏō - "to transform"
WM transformed - "to change across from one
form to another, metamorphosis"

When I renew my mind by meditating
on the Word, I will be changed.
I will not be like the world; I will
be like Christ - I will be in the
will of God.
"Do not adopt the external and
fleeting fashion of this world, but
be transformed in your inmost
nature."
Word Meanings in the New Testament

CHAPTER 5

Step Four:
Draw the
Application

The Word
is God
speaking to you.

Drawing the application is the most difficult skill to practice. Sometimes it is painful because the act of application requires going against our own desires and enacting God's desires for our life. However, the encouraging outcome of meditation is that the longer we meditate, God's will becomes our will. Isaiah 55:8 says, "'For My thoughts are not your thoughts, nor are your ways My ways,' says the LORD." We naturally do not think God's thoughts or want his ways. Yet, meditating on God's Word brings our thoughts and ways into harmony with his thoughts and ways.

In applying Scriptures to our lives, there are three important steps to remember: Use them every day, speak the verses when tempted, and sense the reality of the Word.

USE THE SCRIPTURES EVERY DAY

I have heard friends and well-known speakers testify how quoting one verse changed their lives. Think how much more several verses, chapters, and books will create change.

One hot July morning, in the midst of a carefree summer atmosphere, I awoke feeling grumpy at the world and everyone in it. Immediately, I revealed my true feelings to my family, starting with my husband. He left for work earlier than usual that day—self-preservation. Since our youngest daughter was the only human left in the house, I proceeded to express displeasure to her. She retreated to her bedroom and closed the door. Only our dog was left. When I told him I didn't like the way he made a mess when he ate, he hid from me.

As I was straightening up the kitchen, with very loud sound effects and grumblings to myself, the convicting thought entered my mind: *I hadn't memorized or meditated on any new Scriptures for two weeks*. I had just been repeating verses I already knew. Reluctantly, I decided to take a look at the verses I should have been working on (though I didn't want to see what they said because I was certain they would fit my life).

The first reference was Romans 6:1: "Shall we continue in sin . . . ?" Ouch! The Scriptures didn't need to be that sharp. I had known better than to choose to be grumpy when I awakened that morning. And I didn't have to continue with those attitudes or actions now. So I sat down immediately and began to memorize and meditate on those verses. It's amazing how smoothly the rest of the week went, once I began to turn to Scripture every day.

SPEAK THE VERSES WHEN TEMPTED

There are always lessons to be learned in this life, and, occasionally, there are near-disaster experiences. But I hope and pray that in all the experiences I have gone through—even the flood incident—I have learned all the lessons to be learned from adversity. I don't want to live through those times again to know how to respond properly in danger and temptation. I want to learn my lessons the first time around.

Through memorization and meditation our instincts change. We can respond to hurts, storms, and enticements with trust and righteousness when we know the truth of the Scripture for our lives. Many fall away because they cannot relate the truth of the Word to their daily lives. But Psalm 119:105 reassures us with, "Your word is a lamp to my feet and a light to my path."

Driving at night in the Seattle area when it's foggy and rainy is quite an adventure. Rain lashes the windshield, the road looms shadowy, and it's impossible to see where you're going. But the highway department has provided raised lane markers between lanes to help guide drivers. If you drive over these markers, you're jarred by the bumps, and you know you're driving into someone else's lane—and possible destruction.

God's Word helps us as we meditate to know whether we're weaving over into the wrong lane of life. It is a guide in the daytime as well as the nighttime.

When Jesus was tempted in the wilderness (as told in Matt. 4), he quoted Scripture to confront every temptation. His instinctive reaction was to use the Word against the enemy. If you memorize and meditate, it will be easy for you to train yourself to speak the Word when you are tempted either to wrong thinking or to wrong actions. Romans 8:31 reads, "What then shall we say to these things?" Paul didn't use *think*, but *say*. Declare appropriate verses out loud to situations whenever possible, as Jesus did. For example, you might say Romans 12:2 (to yourself if others are present) when instructed by a boss to be dishonest or when friends pressure you to partake of activities you think are wrong according to Scripture. In both of these instances, Scripture will give you resolve and strength to stand firm on your convictions.

STEP FOUR: DRAW THE APPLICATION

SENSE THE REALITY OF THE WORD

As you sense the reality of the Word, the characters of the Bible will seem true-to-life. When you meditate on someone's writing, you learn a lot about the writer, getting to know him or her. For instance, when you meditate on the Gospels of John or Luke, you will come to think of the writers as your friends. Most of all, you'll become acquainted with the Lord in a new way.

At Christmastime, memorize and meditate on the Christmas story, and at Eastertime, the Easter story for reality of the Word during those seasons.

At night, quote verses as your last thoughts before sleep and notice how the Word gives you restful sleep. Upon waking in the morning quote verses before thinking any other thoughts and experience confidence for your day.

Sense the Scriptures at work in your life. No longer will you be like a child "tossed to and fro," as in Ephesians 4:14, or like the tumble weeds that bounce across the prairies. They have no root system, so they roll wherever the wind blows them. Some even become hopelessly entangled in barbed wire fences against their own will, never to roam again. Instead, you will be rooted and grounded in Christ.

As you use the Scriptures every day, speak the verses when tried or tempted, and sense the reality of the Word, you may wish to make additional notes on your index cards under "applications." Feel free to use more than one card for a verse. However, as you find yourself continuously finding new applications, you may wish to start a journal to record the ongoing story of your growth in and discovery of Christ.

CHAPTER 6

Step Five:
Do It

You are

propelled

by the Word.

In our life we develop habits—some good, some bad. When the alarm rings every morning, we are usually alert to its demand. When God calls us to meditation every day, how do we respond?

We usually do have legitimate excuses, just as the banquet guests did in Jesus' parable in Luke 14:15–20. They gave good reasons for not attending the feast they were summoned to: One had to inspect his real estate; one had to try out recently purchased oxen; and another had just been married. They, however, missed the banquet. Will we?

PLAN MEMORIZE AND MEDITATE AS YOUR PRIORITY

God is a jealous God (see Exodus 20:5). He is either first in our lives, or he is nothing at all. We constantly need to refine our priorities and establish habits that will help us to live faithfully by these priorities. We will discuss several of these habits, or practices, in this chapter.

MAKE YOUR SCHEDULE

In finding priorities, the first thing to select is a memorization and meditation time. This will be different for everyone. If you leap out of bed in the morning singing, morning may be your best time. But if you move slowly in the morning, you'll do your most creative meditating around the middle of the day or in the evening.

Some suggestions for a memorize and meditate time are first thing in the morning, during break times at work, during your lunch hour, immediately

---

STEP FIVE: DO IT

---

after work, in the early evening, or just before going to bed. Choose a specified period for memorization and meditation every day.

Take a few minutes every week to plan priorities. Don't say you'll find the time; *make* the time. When you say you can't find opportunity for memorization and meditation are you saying, "I don't have time for God"? If your life is so structured that you don't have time, you're too busy. A good rule to remember is: fit your life around Memorize and Meditate. Don't try to fit Memorize and Meditate into your life.

It has been discovered that singles and childless couples have about forty hours of leisure, dual-career parents have about twenty hours of leisure, and senior citizens have over forty hours of leisure every week. We fill this free time with many temporary occupations without lasting results: The lawn needs mowing, the groceries always need purchasing, and the mountains are invariably calling to us for exploration. But the benefits of meditation will last for eternity.

Parents, it might be good to consider that when we read, study, and discuss the Bible as a priority in our home, our children will follow the pattern we set for them. They are the mirrors of our lives.

Another important point to consider as you plan your time for memorization and meditation is that life changes. Life goes in cycles: moving to a new town, getting a new job, starting a family, kids going off to school. All of these changes call for readjustment and reorganization of priorities. Realize that every month and every year will not be the same. Be careful of making excuses. It may be necessary to rededicate yourself to this program repeatedly.

Use Memorize and Meditate as Your Study and Devotional Time. This program will give you a consistency that will thrill you as you realize *every day* you are building more and more of the Scriptures into your life. Never again will you be in a quandary about where to study or have devotions.

As it's not possible to study the whole Bible at one time, and you can meditate in only one place at a time, it doesn't matter whether you're not reading and studying in other parts of the Bible, unless you have the time and desire to do so. The key is to concentrate on one portion of Scripture at a time.

Put Forth the Effort. What you put into memorization and meditation is what you get out of it. The Bible teaches us about the principle of giving and receiving in Mark 4. Whatever measure we give out will be the measure that will return to us again. If you put in diligent and consistent effort, you can expect results. If you continue faithfully in meditation, even when you hit a dry spell, you'll be amazed in the long run at the subtle and gradual changes that have taken place in your life.

Today we want everything to be instant. But consider how long it takes a beautiful pearl to form within an oyster—two to three long years. It will take much more time and patience to develop the pearls of our spirits and characters.

SET YOUR GOALS

Another important step in establishing your priorities is deciding each week how many verses you will be able to learn. Be realistic about your goals. It's important for your self-esteem that you achieve the goals you have set. You may have a fairly open week and can spend time on five verses. Your next week might be much busier, so you'll be able to allow time for only two verses. If your schedule becomes more hectic than you anticipated and you are unable to reach your goal, don't be discouraged. Just pick up the verses the next week. If all your weeks become too busy, reexamine your priorities.

You are not competing with anyone. Only you will be able to determine your pace for memorizing and meditating.

If you were to take a trip by car from Boston to Seattle on Interstate 90, you would have a 3,000-mile journey. It seems overwhelming when you look at the whole, but when you break it down, it becomes attainable.

The 3,000-mile trip can be likened to a book or chapter you have chosen for memorizing and meditating. The towns along the way are your weekly goals. Just as you drive one mile at a time, so also you learn one phrase or one verse at a time. And before you know it, you've arrived at the destination.

What follows is a suggested weekly guide you can use in your memorizing and meditating. The first day of your week for memorization and meditation can be on any day of the week. For example, you could start your memorization and meditation with Wednesday as your first day, and insert the sixth and seventh days over the weekend. Then continue with the fourth and fifth days on Monday and Tuesday.

Also, you may memorize all your verses the first day and review and research the rest of the days. Some people like to look up all their words on the first day and concentrate on memory and application on the rest of the days.

Vary the guide to meet your needs, but be sure to have a regular memorization and meditation time five days a week. For as little as fifteen minutes a day, five days a week, you can successfully follow the Memorize and Meditate program.

SUGGESTED WEEKLY GUIDE

First Day—15 minutes

- Start with prayer.
- Write out two to five cards.
- Memorize first verse.
- Research unknown words.
- Write personal application on cards.

Second Day—15 minutes

- Start with prayer.
- Memorize second verse.
- Research unknown words.
- Write personal application on cards.

Third Day—15 minutes

- Start with prayer.
- Review memorized verses or memorize third verse.
- Additional research if desired or research unknown words.
- Write personal application on cards.

Fourth Day—15 minutes

- Start with prayer.
- Review memorized verses or memorize fourth verse.

STEP FIVE: DO IT

- Additional research if desired or research unknown words.
- Write personal application on cards.

Fifth Day—15 minutes

- Start with prayer.
- Review memorized verses or memorize fifth verse.
- Additional research if desired or research unknown words.
- Write personal application on cards.

Sixth Day—Quote all verses in current chapter.

Seventh Day—Quote all verses in current chapter.

PRAY

Sometimes what we discover in our meditation can hit us like a bolt of lightning. Other times the process will seem difficult—maybe too practical—and dull. If this happens, there are four things to consider:

- **Are you spending time in prayer with meditation?**
- **Are you clearing your mind for meditation?**
- **Are you relying on the Holy Spirit to teach you?**
- **Are you trusting the Word to do its work?**

Begin Each Memorize and Meditate Session with Prayer. Prayer is effective in any posture, lying, sitting, or kneeling. Start your time of memorizing and meditating with prayer wherever you are and, before you know it, prayer and meditation will mesh together as one.

Ask God to assist you in the Memorize and Meditate program. He will quickly help you because this is something he wants you to do; this is his basic will for your life every day.

Empty Your Mind of Cares and Fill It with the Word. Cut through the clutter. By an act of the will, as you throw out the problems, you will open yourself to exciting truths with more creativity in every area of your life.

Learn of the Holy Spirit. John 14:26 says, "But the Helper, the Holy Spirit . . . will teach you all things, and bring to your remembrance all things that I said to you." The Holy Spirit will open up the Scriptures to you and will bring verses to memory— even verses you learned years ago—and meditative thoughts to mind when they are needed in living, teaching, or counseling.

Trust in the Quickening Power of God's Word. Listen for the Scriptures you are memorizing and meditating in the minister's sermons, verses in Sunday school lessons, and verses in Bible studies. You will begin to see new applications of the Scriptures in your life. Then, the Word will be alive for you, and you will become alive through the Word. God merely spoke the Word, and all creation came into being. As Romans 4:17b states: "God, who gives life to the dead, and calls those things which do not exist as though they did . . . ," he can take nothing and make it into something. God gives life to our hearts, souls, and minds when they are dead.

It is Christ who gives us life, power, and strength to

work out our goals to overcome distressing pressure that comes from without and within. In his words are spirit and life.

RELAX

Many cultures around the world have "siesta" periods every day for resting, thinking, or relaxing. When you're not used to this, you may feel uncomfortable taking time for it, and you'll catch yourself dwelling on all the things you need to do. But stay with it. This special quiet time is for your strength, so there's no need to feel uptight about taking the time for memorization and meditation. Consciously make yourself relax.

Free Yourself of Stress to Improve Your Memory. Stress is a growing problem today, and stress management lies at the root of physical, emotional, and spiritual health. A small amount of stress gives us a sense of mental alertness, high motivation, and improved memory. But when we are in distress, we experience an overload of stress, which causes fatigue, irritability, and diminished memory and can lead to illness.

Occasionally, we bring undue strain on ourselves by trying to measure up to expectations others may have of us that aren't in tune with our gifts or temperament. This produces anxiety in us to varying degrees.

Meditation will relieve the stress we experience in our daily lives, such as tension from our jobs or families or various relationships. Start by imagining yourself in meditation, and soon it will be a reality.

Anyone can develop a consistent meditation program.

Start an Exercise Program. Since I started working out on a rebound exercise unit, I realize how much physical and spiritual training go hand in hand. When I am disciplined physically, then I'm diligent spiritually. Regular exercise relieves stress, makes you feel alive, and sharpens the mind. I'm not advocating that you become an exercise fanatic. But everyone can be involved in some form of exercise— walking, swimming, bicycling—for as little as ten minutes a day. Doctors tell us that physical exertion increases the flow of blood to the brain, which increases mental powers. Thus, not only will you feel the difference in your body, but you'll see the evidence in your meditation as well.

THINK POSITIVELY

"I Can." When you say you can't, you can't, and you immediately set up a mental block for any new learning. Some people tell me they can't memorize and meditate. Of course they can't; their mental outlook hinders them.

Researchers have discovered that negative attitudes also cause "the blues," which can distort your memory and your perspective. Negative people see evil in everything. I heard a story about one negative person who threw away his alphabet cereal one morning because he saw a dirty word in it. Or how about the young man who lost his job in advertising because he didn't have anything good to say about the product?

STEP FIVE: DO IT

In order to memorize and meditate, we need one of the basic skills of survival—positive thinking. Survival courses teach that a positive mental attitude is essential for keeping alive.

Philippians 4:13 says, "I can do all things through Christ who strengthens me." Nothing is impossible. You can, through Christ, memorize and meditate on whole chapters or books.

Be Careful of Pride.   Pride generates negative response. We have to be tactful about not intimidating others who are not involved in memorizing and meditating.

A well-known minister made this comment: "A Christian is in the greatest danger not at his weak points but at his strong ones. Where we are strong we are also off guard."[1]

EXERCISE THE MIND

Your mind is like a muscle, and it is strengthened by exercise. If your mind is untrained, it will be necessary for you to expand its capacity for memorizing. Recall verses day and night. Also, recall as much of the verses or chapter as possible before checking yourself in your Bible. This stretches your mind.

Memorize Various Daily Lists.   Memorize telephone numbers, grocery lists, things-to-do-today lists. Make yourself recall the numbers and the items on the lists to develop your memory. You will be amazed, after practice, how easy it has become for you to remember information and how much more easily you can memorize and meditate.

THE
MAINTENANCE
PLAN

CHAPTER 7

Find
a Partner

You are

upheld

by the Word.

When I have tried to memorize and meditate without a partner, it hasn't worked. Most of us, in order to continue the Memorize and Meditate program, will need a partner.

The ideal partner is an acquaintance. Intimate friends or family members are not always best because of your familiarity with them. But they cannot be ruled out as a possibility.

If you sense that your partner doesn't want to continue with Memorize and Meditate, discuss it with him or her. Be diplomatic. You can't force your partner to want to continue, but you may be able to help him or her over a temporary difficulty so he or she does want to continue. If all efforts fail, the Lord will help you find another partner.

When we moved to a different city, I didn't have a partner the first month we were there. One day I became desperate and told the Lord I couldn't live another day without someone for a Memorize and Meditate partner. That night Norma, one of the ladies of our church, asked me to share with her the method I had found for memorizing and meditating. God had been speaking to her about being in his Word in a deeper way. She has been my faithful partner ever since. God answers our prayers before we even pray them.

The following five guidelines help to make the partner concept successful.

1. CALL ONCE A WEEK

Call your partner every week at a pre-appointed time to listen to each other's verses. I can't emphasize enough the importance of this step. This makes the whole program effective.

Ask the Lord to help you find a time convenient for both of you. I call my partner every Saturday morning between nine and ten A.M. We prayed about a calling time, and this has worked out great for us.

You and your partner can take turns initiating the call, or one of you can make the call every week. You may, instead of making a telephone call, want to meet a few minutes before or after a church service, if you attend the same church, or meet for breakfast, lunch, or coffee once a week. Do what works best.

2. KEEP YOUR CALL BRIEF

If you are a talker and like to make long telephone calls, this is not the time to do it. Remember, the purpose of this call is for Memorize and Meditate. If you get in the habit of bringing up other topics, the temporal will soon crowd out the spiritual ministry. If you need to talk to your partner about other things, call at another time.

During this call, say your current verses for your partner. Unless you have an agreement to say all the verses of your chapter, it is not necessary to say all the verses of your chapter every week; just quote new memory work. Then you can make some brief comments you think might be a blessing to your partner concerning some of your meditative thoughts. But be careful of sharing too much. Some things should be kept between yourself and God. Also, be careful of using this time for unloading problems on your partner. This can destroy the uplift of the Scriptures.

3. INDICATE CORRECTIONS

Have your Bible open, ready to check your partner as he or she says the verses. You could also have a paper and pencil available to jot down errors your partner makes. When your partner is finished, tell him or her in an encouraging way of changes that need to be made. Be careful of nitpicking. Then, have your partner correct you when you have finished saying your verses.

4. BE FAITHFUL

Faithfulness will benefit you and your partner. Never make excuses to your partner when she or he calls unless you have an emergency. Putting your partner off is not being fair to your partner or to yourself. If you have made a commitment, follow through. You will feel strength the rest of the day.

5. PRAY, INSPIRE, ENCOURAGE

You will, at times, struggle with this commitment. You will *need* each others' prayers, inspiration, and encouragement through the good times as well as the discouraging times. Consider this: You are helping each other build for eternity. It is worth the time and the effort.

◆ CHAPTER 8 ◆

Plan for
Review

You are

sustained

by the Word.

It's one thing to know how to memorize and meditate, but it is quite another to continue the program and to continue to remember those first verses you memorized.

Even if you have never used a system of review, the Word will remain in the memory forever. However, review keeps the verses fresh in your memory. On the next few pages, I have outlined a plan you may find helpful.

For every chapter:

1. Write in your Bible the date you start and the date you finish memorizing a chapter. This will be of interest to you as you continue to memorize and meditate. (In the following material, treat the half chapters or segments of chapters mentioned in chapter 3 as whole chapters.)

2. Enter in your Bible a one- or two-word caption summarizing each chapter. It may be a word no one else would choose for that chapter, but it needs to be a key thought that will trigger your memory about the entire content of the chapter. Sometimes it is necessary to break down the chapter because of a shift in subject matter, so perhaps use another word caption halfway through the chapter. Examples of one-word captions for the first few chapters of Romans are:

Chapter 1—Sin
Chapter 2—Law
Chapter 3—Justification

Memorize these captions for each chapter and recall them to memory about once a month for all the chapters you have learned since starting Memorize and Meditate.

PLAN FOR REVIEW

---

3. Underline verses that have special significance to you. By experience, we know the importance of underlining verses so we can find them quickly when we need them. This also helps to imprint the verse in our minds.

4. Review word for word, once a week, the previous chapter you learned when starting a new chapter; repeat this for three consecutive weeks, then discontinue. For instance, if you just finished memorizing the first chapter of Philippians, as you start with the first few verses of chapter 2, review your first chapter at least once, word for word, recalling your meditative thoughts. For the next two weeks, you will quote chapter 1 again, as you continue to memorize in Philippians. After your third week of doing this, it will not be necessary for you to recite the first chapter word for word unless you desire. But it is necessary to quote perfectly as much as you have memorized in the current chapter.

SCHEDULING YOUR REVIEW TIME

Choose a special day or set aside one day from your Memorize and Meditate schedule for review: When one to eleven chapters are memorized, review once bimonthly. When twelve to twenty-five chapters are memorized, review once a month. When twenty-six to fifty-one chapters are memorized, review once biweekly. When fifty-two or more chapters are memorized, review once a week. In each review time:

Spend fifteen minutes.
Review *only one chapter*.

THE MAINTENANCE PLAN

Give attention to your one-word caption for that chapter.

Read through the chapter.

Take special note of underlined verses.

Make use of cards to refresh your memory as to what your meditations were.

CREATING A REVIEW CARD

Having a review card helps you to be consistent with your review and helps you to retain meditative thoughts. The sample review card below helps to illustrate how your card should look.

Schedule 3

1990   Review time—Sunday afternoon

Philippians 1—January 7

Philippians 2—January 21

Philippians 3—February 4

1. Write in the year at the top left-hand corner of one of your index cards.

2. Select a review time and record it at the top mid-

dle of the card. Find a time you are certain you can be faithful to. It may be Saturday night, Sunday afternoon, or any weekday.

3. Record the schedule you will be following on the top right-hand corner of the card.

4. Below the headings, list the chapter and the date of review when you have finished your review.

CHAPTER 9

Enjoy
the Benefits

You are

recreated

by the Word.

If someone offered to give you a map to help you find buried treasure, would you accept it? Of course you would. In fact, you would quickly make plans to find that treasure and benefit from it.

Treasures are available to you from the Word of God, via the map of Memorize and Meditate. With the five D's for the Memorize and Meditate program—Decide the Method, Determine the Location, Discover the Content, Draw the Application, and Do It—and with a partner and a plan for review, you can enjoy increased intelligence, improved health, stimulated creativity, relief from stress, attained potential, consistent devotions, and eternal treasure.

INCREASED INTELLIGENCE

When you seek God's wisdom first, increased intelligence can follow. Students who memorize and meditate often testify that their grades improve from C and B averages to A averages.

You gain not only wisdom, but also love, stability, and righteousness from memorization and meditation. The attributes of God will be demonstrated in your life as well.

IMPROVED HEALTH

It is an established fact that avoidance of disease starts in the mind. What you think can make you well or sick.

You will enjoy improved health as you allow Scriptures to govern your thoughts, and you will no longer be controlled by impure motives and emotions or harmful anxieties.

STIMULATED CREATIVITY

Have you truly discovered what God has planned for you? Your niche? Have you recognized the purpose that is entirely in turn with your gifts and your inner self? Do you have a sense of completeness?

Spend some time with God every day in memorization and meditation, communing with him and thinking his thoughts, and you will be surprised at the results. God's creativity will abound in your life, beyond what you ever dared to desire.

RELIEF FROM STRESS

Acquire faith and peace for every day and reserve for emergencies. A wise person has said, "Sometimes God calms the storms, and sometimes he calms his child during the storm." You will have the peace to endure whatever comes your way.

I experienced a "storm" firsthand one beautiful spring afternoon in the Black Hills. Seated in a comfortable recliner, meditating on Ephesians 3:16 ("That He would grant you, according to the riches of His glory, to be strengthened with might through His Spirit in the inner man") and drinking from the mountain scene that stretched out before me through the picture windows of our living room, my spirit revived. The grandfather clock chimed. JoAnn needed to be picked up from school. *If I hurry I won't be too late,* I thought.

I bounced out of the chair, picked up my handbag and keys, tore down the stairs to the garage, got into the car, put the key in the ignition, started the car, gazed into the rearview mirror, and backed out—

through the garage door. I was shattered, and so was the door.

Karen, who was in her room, ran downstairs and gawked with disbelief, "What happened?"

"I don't want to talk about it," I said through clenched teeth as we both started to pick up the pieces of glass for the garbage can and stacked wood for the fireplace.

As my sanity returned, I sent Karen off to school to pick up JoAnn and went upstairs to call my husband at his office to prepare him for what he would face when he came home.

Unbelievably, I reached him right away. "Honey, you'll never guess what happened." I started to cry (crying always helps a little). "I thought this only happened to people in books, but," sniff, sniff, "I backed out through the garage door."

A long pause, then . . . laughter.

I had prepared myself for everything but that. How could he laugh at a time like this?

After our conversation, I slinked to the garage to cover my handiwork before the neighbors could see. I put up the remains of the door to hide it, and as I did, more glass and wood fell. The girls were now home and helped me collect all the bits.

Just then, our church elder's wife drove by.

"Aren't you going to wave, Mom?" JoAnn asked.

"No! Don't move. She may not see us."

Stress—this was stress. All I longed for right then was for the last half hour of my life to be bleeped from time.

It took a few days for me to recover. But I had a reserve for the days following this "emergency." When the verse I had been meditating on began to take effect, I sensed a strengthening inside. Strength for the day. Strength to laugh about it in the future.

ATTAINED POTENTIAL

You will reach your potential not when you are dependent upon people, talents, and environment, but when you place your confidence in Christ for that capacity. Philippians 1:6 tells us: "Being confident of this very thing, that He who has begun a good work in you will complete it." God will complete you when you avail yourself of his Word for development. With this confidence, you can face and overcome the obstacles to reach your potential.

CONSISTENT DEVOTIONS

The Memorize and Meditate program is a solution for a consistent, devotional time with the Lord. It is a consistent way to commune with God, feed on his Word, and find answers to life's problems.

For the first time in my life I am *feeding* on the Word. "Your words were found, and I ate them" (Jer. 15:16).

The only creature I know of who has not benefited from feeding on the Word was our dog Skippy. He ate the entire book of Philippians out of my Bible. Instead of his disposition improving, he got mean. We had to get rid of him.

ETERNAL TREASURE

A story is told of a long-ago Persian, Ali Hafed,[1] who lived not far from the River Indus. He owned a very large farm with gardens, vineyards, and grainfields. He was very wealthy and content—until he heard about diamonds. Then he became discontent. Ali Hafed wanted, indeed craved, a diamond mine and what it could buy him. So he sold his farm, collected his money, left his family with a neighbor, and went in search of a diamond mine. He wandered the world searching . . . searching . . . until all his money was spent and he was in rags, poverty, and wretchedness. Finally, in despair, he cast himself into the sea.

The man who purchased Ali Hafed's farm led his camel into the garden to drink one day. As the camel put its nose into the shallow water, Ali Hafed's successor noticed a curious flash of light from the white sands of the stream—a beautiful diamond. Shortly, a whole diamond mine was discovered, the Golcanda mine, which produced the largest jewels on earth.

If only Ali Hafed had known about the diamond mine. If only he had found the treasure right in his own backyard.

In your home there is treasure: the Bible. With a little digging, you will find the benefits for your life. You need not search the world. It is in your Bible. In your home.

ENJOY THE BENEFITS

How to Teach Kids Memorize and Meditate

The best way to guide children spiritually is to help them learn the teachings and principles of the Bible through memorization and meditation. Teach them to judge everything by Scripture, so they will realize that all other ground is inconsistent.

There are fifty-two weeks in a year, and a child attends school from kindergarten through twelfth grade, thirteen years. If a child learns just one verse of Scripture a week for thirteen years, he or she will have learned 676 verses before he or she graduates from high school. And with only a little extra work here are some other possibilities:

A child could learn the entire book of Mark, which has 678 verses, or several chapters or passages of Scripture, such as:

The Sermon on the Mount	111 verses
Ephesians	155 verses
Philippians	104 verses
1 Timothy	113 verses
James	108 verses
1 John	105 verses
	696 verses

Planting this amount of Scripture into your children's minds will help them to develop positive actions and attitudes. You will, indeed, be "training up your child."

You will find the Memorize and Meditate for Kids program discussed in detail in my book *The Bible Verse Book*. This program includes activities you and your child can do together as the child learns the Scriptures. The five D's for children, explained in this book, are the same as those for adults, with a few changes. The basic steps are included here.

BEFORE YOU BEGIN

Choose a Bible translation your child can appreciate and understand. It's important that your child use one Bible throughout her or his years of memorizing and meditating. So start with a translation the child won't outgrow.

As with the adult Memorize and Meditate program, children may use an index card system for their Memorize and Meditate program. Give each of your children cards for his or her memory work. (See sample card on page 49.)

Have your child write one verse per card and record any word meanings you and your child discover. Let your child write any thoughts or applications for each verse. (You may need to help her or him write the verses and meanings, if the child is preschool aged.)

Be sensitive to your child's learning capacity and select only the number of verses you think he or she can comfortably handle each week.

One grandmother told me that her son and his wife didn't seem to have time to start her granddaughter with memorization and meditation, so she has started it with the child. The grandfather printed out the verses on the cards, and both grandparents became involved in teaching Scriptures to their granddaughter. What a great way to establish bonds with grandchildren!

Keep the cards of the current verses visible by placing them on the refrigerator with magnets or tacking them on the child's bulletin board. If you want to protect the cards so that they will last longer, you may cover them with plastic recipe card covers; then, throw the plastic away when the verse has been learned.

Assemble a card file box for each child to store the cards in when he or she has finished memorizing and meditating on each verse. Before you file the cards, record the date your child completed the work.

DECIDE THE METHOD

Have your child choose from the five suggested methods for memorizing, which follow, the one he or she is comfortable with.

Method 1: Repetition. Memorizing is easy for kids. Their minds are fresh and quick. And the most common way children learn information and facts is by repetition.

Be sure they say the verse aloud three times, visualize the verse (if they're older), and write the verse three times.

Method 2: Form Acronyms. This is particularly effective to use for verses that list several things.

Method 3: Association. If your child does not respond to repetition, teach her or him to memorize by association, relating each verse to a picture you or your child draws to depict each verse. Be sure to keep the picture simple.

Method 4: Record on Cassettes. For children who enjoy listening to cassettes, record portions of Scripture so they can listen to the tapes throughout the day. It's a positive reinforcement for them to hear

Dad's or Mom's voice during the day. And if they play the Scripture tape just before they go to sleep at night, they'll sleep better and perhaps learn the verse more easily.

Method 5: Sing Scripture. Encourage children who enjoy singing to make up songs using the words of verses that are special to them.

DETERMINE THE LOCATION

Ask the Lord to guide you to the portion of Scripture each of your children needs. It is less work for you if all your children are working on the same Scriptures at the same time. However, there are times when one child may need a different Scripture because of his or her specific needs for encouragement or instruction or because he or she is not at the same level as the other children. For age-appropriate Scripture references refer to *The Bible Verse Book.*

DISCOVER THE CONTENT

1. Research key words in the dictionary and, if your child can write, have the child write the definitions on index cards.

You may not want to use a dictionary with pre-schoolers. Instead, use examples to teach word meanings. To teach the meaning of the word *kind,* you might demonstrate politeness. When a sibling takes advantage of the younger child, show him or her how to be "kind" in return. However, you should use a dictionary along with active experience to teach word meanings to children aged six to twelve. A teen can use a concordance, as well as a dictionary and interactive discussion with you, to discover word meanings.

2. Simplify thoughts and explanations for each age level. Take an active part in sharing and discussing the verses with your children so they may learn to meditate on their own intellectual levels.

3. Insert the child's name in appropriate verses to personalize the verses.

DRAW THE APPLICATION

1. Prompt creative thinking by asking questions, such as: What do you think about this verse? What do you feel about this verse? How can this verse fit into (apply to) your life? Open-ended questions, such as these, affirm your child's ideas and inspire creative thinking. This is a good time for you as a parent to add new ideas in the discussion with your child.

2. Guide each child in relating each verse to life experiences. Limited experience produces limited understanding, so the more experiences your child can have, the better off she or he will be. Use every opportunity during the week to point out, in a casual manner, how the verses your child is learning relate to her or his life. Ask God to help you be alert to living object lessons and trust that the Holy Spirit will enlighten your child's mind to the truth of the Word for application to life. The Holy Spirit speaks and makes Scripture real to a child, too.

Remember that, in order for your children to understand Scriptures, not only must they feel and experience Scripture for themselves, but also they need to see your example. Otherwise, they'll develop a confused picture of what the Bible means. If parents can't live the Word, they shouldn't teach the Word.

3. Incorporate applications into your prayer time with each child. This aids the child in applying instruction of the Scriptures immediately. For example, if your child learns the verse "Be kind : . . ," he or she can ask God to help him or her be kind to brothers and sisters and neighbors. This specific prayer effects specific answers.

DO IT

1. Schedule Memorize and Meditate Times with Your Children. Choose the time that fits best with everyone's schedules:

- **Work on memorization in the morning and meditation during the day and in the evening.**
- **If you drive your children to school, work on memorization and meditation on the way to and from school.**
- **If your children are old enough to memorize and meditate on their own, you may want to schedule a special family time when you discuss Scripture and answer your children's questions; perhaps on a Sunday afternoon or evening.**

If you have a tentative schedule, you'll need to create time for memorizing and meditating. The effort you put forth will be worth it; however, this time does need to be a priority for it to be successful.

2. Pray for the Lord's Help. Ask the Lord to help you as a parent to guide and instruct your children.

Use part of memorization and meditation time for prayer, especially in the evening. Many parents go through a routine of saying prayers with their children before they go to sleep, so using this time will be familiar to both of you. Many children have trouble sleeping and experience nightmares, so memorization and meditation will bring peace to them as nothing else will.

3. Relax with Your Children. Lie down on the bed or curl up in a chair with them. For Memorize and Meditate to be successful, there has to be a relaxed atmosphere. Children respond and learn more quickly when "it's fun." Avoid pressuring them. Use this time to get to know them better and to guide them into knowing God.

4. Be Positive About Memorize and Meditate. Encourage your children in their progress. Sometimes children will make mistakes when saying their verses for you. When this happens, repeat the verse in the correct form without drawing attention to the error. You will be modeling the correct version in a positive manner that encourages communication and does not dampen their desire. If your children are struggling with the program, find a different method for memorizing or a unique way of meditating. But always keep your comments positive. Early childhood specialists say: "Positive comments from significant adults provide important guideposts for children's behavior . . . focus on improvement . . . avoid comparisons or competition."[1] These guidelines are necessary for an enthusiastic response from your children. Memorization and meditation can't be like "drill time." Children will always associate the emotions they had during memorization and meditation with the Word of God; therefore, make these moments cheerful and pleasant.

EXTRA HELPS

1. Use a Five-Day Schedule. On the weekend, give Memorize and Meditate a rest unless an opportune moment occurs for casually teaching the meaning or application of a verse your child is working on.

2. Use Incentives. Incentives are not bribery but rewards for behavior, which reassure your child that the content of the verses they are learning merit value at home. As long as rewards are necessary, feel comfortable about using them to reinforce your values to your child.

Make the rewards appropriate for the amount of verses learned and for your child's age: a piece of candy for one verse, a picnic for a month of verses, a shopping trip for six months of verses, and so on. Below are a few other incentives arranged by age group:

Ages 2 to 5

a sticker	candy	cookie
ice cream	inexpensive toy	coloring book
first Bible	money	new book
a picnic	help Mom bake	trip to zoo
stay up later		
shopping trip with Mom or Dad		

Ages 6 to 12

new book or cassette   special bike ride
new clothing item   slumber party at home
toy model   lunch with Mom and Dad
money
attend a sporting event with parents
permission to go to a friend's house

Ages 13 to 18

new "fad" item   have a friend stay overnight
new book or cassette   family car for one day
Strong's Concordance   item for collection
money   leather-bound Bible
privilege to stay up late one night (at home!)
Dad or Mom will do one of the child's chores
dinner with Dad or Mom at an upscale restaurant

If I were to poll parents who read this book, I'm
sure the response would be that you want the best for
your children. We teach our children habits for good
health and cleanliness. We send them to school to
learn. Any extracurricular activity they desire, and
we can afford, is theirs—music, sports, hobbies,
travel, computers. However, parents have said to me,
"I'm not going to force my children to attend church
or make them read the Bible. I don't want to make
them rebellious."

When they are encouraged to do so with the right
spirit, children rarely become rebellious about going
to church or learning the Word. It is the child who

does not learn faithfulness in church attendance and a love for the Scriptures who has no foundation of values and will, in the end, become rebellious.

The bottom line is if you live the way you expect your children to live, they will not depart from your spiritual training and will grow up to respect and revere you and the God you serve.

How to Start a Memorize and Meditate Club

The purpose of a Memorize and Meditate Club is for members to encourage one another in the commitment to memorizing and meditating on the Word. As the Scripture states: "Let us hold fast the confession of our hope without wavering. . . . And let us consider one another in order to stir up love and good works, not forsaking the assembling of ourselves together . . . but exhorting one another" (Heb. 10:23–25).

Members of your Sunday school class or your neighbors, co-workers, any group of business or professional people, women's club (social or church), couple's group, or single's group could be effectively transformed into a Memorize and Meditate Club.

The following pages list some guidelines for such a club. Feel free to alter them to fit the needs of your particular group.

CLUB FORMATS

Before you begin to meet regularly, your group will want to choose the format you'll use for your weekly meetings. There are two basic formats, or types, of Memorize and Meditate Clubs. First, you can organize a study group in which all members of the club memorize and meditate on the same portion of Scripture. At each meeting, members contribute to the unfolding of truths and applications from those verses for comprehensive analysis.

The other type of group is a diversified group in which all members of the group select their own Scriptures. During the meeting, the sharing is varied, and the results are inspirational.

Whether you decide on a study group for comprehensive analysis or a diversified group for inspiration, either method is very successful.

ORGANIZATION

When starting a Memorize and Meditate Club, contact all persons interested to inform them of the first meeting to decide how the club will be organized. The first order of business is to choose a leader. A club leader may be:

- **Appointed by informal agreement of the majority,**
- **Voted on formally by the majority, or**
- **Appointed by the senior pastor or Christian education minister (if the club is held in the church).**

The leader then finds the general concensus of the majority as to how the club will be organized. If your group decides to remain relatively unstructured, you need not keep records. But if your club decides on a structured organization, the leader may want to use some of the following guidelines.

CLUB LEADER RESPONSIBILITIES

1. Record the Name, Address, and Phone Number of Every Member. Anyone who has read *Memorize and Meditate* and is currently practicing this method may become a member of a Memorize and Meditate Club.

2. Take Attendance at Every Meeting. The leader keeps close contact with all members. If a member has not attended the last two meetings, the leader should write a note or make a personal call to that person to assist with any problems he or she may have.

3. Keep a List of Partners. To help members find partners, place half of the names of the group in a hat and have the other half of the group draw out names. This is similar to what is reported in Acts 1:26, when lots were cast to fill the apostle vacancy. With this method no one can feel left out. Be sure to pray, before the names are drawn, that God will give each person the right partner. Encourage all the members to benefit by having a partner, but remind them that it is not mandatory. Discourage partner changes; however, because people move or drop out, you may need to assist a member in finding a new partner.

4. Record Visitors Attending Each Meeting. Find out if the visitor desires to become a member. (See number one above for membership requirements.)

5. Decide the Time, Place, and Length of Meetings with the Members. Schedule club meetings on the same day once a month or bimonthly as the members determine. Select a meeting place—church, home, office, or restaurant—that is convenient for most of the members. If you serve refreshments, keep them simple so no one has to miss any part of the meeting to prepare refreshments. Keep the meetings short—one to two hours. Short meetings will be better attended.

6. Plan Agenda of Meetings. Try to keep the meetings interesting and varied. At some time during each meeting the leader asks the group to share new ideas for memorizing and meditating and answers any questions regarding the basics of Memorize and Meditate or personal meditations. This is an excellent stretching experience for you as leader.

Allow the most time in the meeting for member sharing. Encourage everyone to tell some of his or her meditations. What they relate may be just what someone else in the club may need to hear; even when members consider their thoughts to be insignificant, they may minister to someone. The sharing may take place either among the whole group or in smaller groups of four to eight persons, depending on the size of your group.

Keep in mind three principles for group sharing:

1. *Be firm.* Don't allow any one person to monopolize all the time.
2. *Never allow doctrinal arguments.* When each member tells what the Scripture means to him or her personally, there need be no argument.
3. *The purpose of the meeting is for memorization and meditation.* Permit only sharing of new methods, meditative thoughts, personal applications, and word meanings.

CLUB SECRETARY RESPONSIBILITIES

If your club desires, or if the leader requests it, the members can appoint or elect a club secretary to assist the leader. The following are suggestions for the secretary.

1. Take attendance at the club meetings.

2. Call every club member a few days before the meeting to remind them of the time and place of the meeting. If the secretary has more than twelve members to call, the club leader may want to form a calling committee. The secretary should record the name and phone number of each member on an index card and divide the cards equally among the calling committee members. They may exchange the cards frequently to keep from calling the same persons all the time.

3. Assist the leader with any mailings to club members.

Most Often
Asked
Questions

Q. If I can't memorize, can I still be involved in Memorize and Meditate?

A. Yes, of course. But the best results for meditating are realized if you memorize. Be sure you don't have a hangup about memorizing that goes back to your school days—tests, grades, competitions, and the like. If you do, put these memories behind you and try memorizing now. Discover that you *can* do it.

Q. What Bible version is best to use for memorizing and meditating?

A. The version you are the most comfortable with. Some popular versions are the *King James Version* (KJV), the *New King James Version* (NKJV), and the *New International Version* (NIV). Choose the one you prefer and stay with it to avoid confusion in your mind as you memorize and meditate.

Q. What should I do if I have trouble memorizing a couple of verses in a chapter?

A. Go on to the next verse. Don't let a difficult verse or group of verses stop you from learning the rest of the chapter and gaining from meditation on the whole chapter.

Q. Is it necessary to learn greetings, farewells, or verses that don't interest me in a chapter?

A. It is best to learn the whole chapter for continuity and self-discipline. Also, be aware that verses you think have no value often have rich treasures when you dig deeply into them in meditation.

MOST OFTEN ASKED QUESTIONS

Q. I have heard many negative things said about meditating. Is it really okay?

A. Scripture meditation is always okay. The Bible speaks often about meditating on the law of the Lord (especially Psalm 119). Joshua 1:8 says that we will be prosperous and successful if we meditate. Don't confuse Scripture meditation with New Age or cult meditation. They're not the same.

Q. What can I do to keep my mind from wandering while I meditate?

A. This is very normal at first. Just bring your mind back to the Scripture verse you started to memorize. However, don't rule out the possibility that, in your wandering thoughts, the Lord may be trying to show you how he wants you to obey the verse you are meditating on. If you are meditating on a verse about hospitality, you may begin to think about how you may fellowship with various people in your church or neighborhood and how and when you can invite them into your home. This is a practical application of Scripture and is a healthy process that occurs in effective meditation.

Q. Can I use the Memorize and Meditate program as my personal Bible study?

A. Yes. Many individuals use this as their daily Bible study.

Q. Can I use a daily journal instead of index cards for my meditations?

A. Yes, if a journal suits you better. Some have found that cards force them to meditate about every verse; others enjoy the freedom of a journal. Use what you like best.

Q. How many verses do I need to learn every week?

A. This is a choice you make at the beginning of your week when you make out your cards, and it may vary from week to week. One week you may learn five verses; the next week you may have time for only two verses. Be careful of discouraging yourself with unrealistic expectations—attempting to memorize too many verses. Try to be consistent, but allow yourself flexibility when you need it. Enjoy your time with the Lord.

Q. Is it necessary to remember everything I've memorized?

A. No, unless you want to. You must make a choice. Do you want to retain everything you've memorized, or do you want to retain the meditations you've gleaned? It's not possible to retain all verses and all meditations unless you have *a lot of time* to spend. To retain your meditations, follow the review plan in chapter 8.

Q. Do I need a partner?

A. No. If you're a self-starter, you probably don't need a partner. The idea of working with a partner is for those who need support and encouragement from someone else.

Q. I would like a partner, but what if I don't make a good partner?

A. Anyone can be a good partner. You simply make or receive one call a week, listen to your partner say his or her verses, and then encourage him or her. There are no other requirements. If a call is missed occasionally, it's all right.

Q. Can my spouse be my partner?

A. Yes, if that is what you both desire. But be sure you don't habitually put other activities before your scheduled weekly memorization and meditation time.

Q. Can my best friend be my partner?

A. Possibly, but if you find it easy to excuse each other and never seem to find time for memorization and meditation, you may need a partner you don't know as well. Some people prefer to find a partner they feel equal to—a friend or acquaintance; others need someone they can look up to, a mentor figure. Find what works for you.

Q. What if my partner learns more verses than I do?

A. You're not in competition with your partner, so never feel intimidated by your partner's progress. Memorize and Meditate is a personal program. You don't want to go so fast in your memorization that you can't keep up with your meditation.

APPENDIX C

Q. What can I do to get back into memorization and meditation if I miss several weeks because of vacation, sickness, or life changes?

A. Here are some positive steps to help you get back into memorization and meditation.

1. **Don't put a guilt trip on yourself. Allow for your humanness. Just start again.**
2. **Recognize the cycles of life. If you have a difficult time doing memorization and meditation in the summertime, recognize it as the lean season and do what you can. Then, in the fall increase the amount of verses you're learning again. Most people have three decision times during the year: September, January, and May. Use these months to reassess your goals for memorization and meditation and to make new starts.**
3. **Start where you left off. If you quit in the middle of a chapter, review the verses you have memorized and then memorize the rest of the chapter.**

Q. How do I become consistent with my memorization and meditation?

A. Find a rhythm that works for you. Forget instruction you've heard about designating specific amounts of time you must spend with the Lord every day. Spend what time you can. If you're erratic, be consistently erratic. For example, if you'd rather spend two or three hours one day a week on memorization and meditation than fifteen minutes every day, then do it. If fifteen minutes, five days a week works for you, do it. The schedule in chapter 6 is there as a guide for you, but you still have to find your rhythm. Consistency also comes with realizing that this program is vital and valuable; that it is essential for stability and positive change in your life.

Q. How can I acquire knowledge of other parts of the Bible if I spend so much time in one chapter or book?

A. This is a lifetime program, and since it is not possible to acquire all knowledge of the Bible quickly, don't worry that you are spending a lot of time in one book. However, if you desire an overview of the Bible, take advantage of the teaching available in your church. Take notes from the pastor's sermons and attend as many classes and Bible studies as you can. Also, use other references, such as commentaries and study Bibles. Then continue your own private time of memorization and meditation. Remember, you can "eat" only a small portion of Scripture at one time.

Q. Can Memorize and Meditate be used in a class or study group?

A. Yes, very successfully. A class or study group can become a support group that brings encouragement to all persons involved.

NOTES

1. COME ALIVE BY THE WORD

1. James Strong, *The New Strong's Exhaustive Concordance of the Bible* (Nashville: Thomas Nelson Publishers, 1984).

2. STEP ONE: DECIDE THE METHOD

1. Jerry Lucas and Harry Lorayne, *The Memory Book* (New York: Stein and Day Publishers, 1974), 23.

3. STEP TWO: DETERMINE THE LOCATION

1. *Strange Stories, Amazing Facts* (New York: The Reader's Digest Association, Inc., 1980), 42-43.

4. STEP THREE: DISCOVER THE CONTENT

1. Laurence Urdang, ed., *The Random House College Dictionary* (New York: Random House, Inc., 1975).

6. STEP FIVE: DO IT

1. Charles Blair with John Sherill and Elizabeth Sherill, *The Man Who Could Do No Wrong* (Lincoln, VA: Chosen Books, 1981), 140.

9. ENJOY THE BENEFITS

1. Russell Conwell, *Acres of Diamonds* (Westwood, NJ: Revell, 1960).

APPENDIX A

1. Amy Driscoll and Randy Hitz, "Practice Encouragement?" *Young Children* (July 1988), 6.